WALCH PUBLISHING

Daily Warm-Ups

VOCABULARY
WORD PLAY

Level II

The classroom teacher may reproduce materials in this book for classroom use only.
The reproduction of any part for an entire school or school system is strictly prohibited.
No part of this publication may be transmitted, stored, or recorded in any form
without written permission from the publisher.

1   2   3   4   5   6   7   8   9   10
ISBN 0-8251-6060-X
Copyright © 2006
J. Weston Walch, Publisher
P.O. Box 658 • Portland, Maine 04104-0658
www.walch.com
Printed in the United States of America

The *Daily Warm-Ups* series is a wonderful way to turn extra classroom minutes into valuable learning time. The 180 quick activities—one for each day of the school year—practice vocabulary skills. These daily activities may be used at the very beginning of class to get students into learning mode, near the end of class to make good educational use of that transitional time, in the middle of class to shift gears between lessons—or whenever else you have minutes that now go unused.

Daily Warm-Ups are easy-to-use reproducibles—simply photocopy the day's activity and distribute it. Or make a transparency of the activity and project it on the board. You may want to use the activities for extra-credit points or as a check on the vocabulary skills that are built and acquired over time.

However you choose to use them, *Daily Warm-Ups* are a convenient and useful supplement to your regular lesson plans. Make every minute of your class time count!

Food Fun

The following sentences are missing two words. The two missing words are spelled the same, but may not have the same meaning. At least one of the words in each pair has to do with food. Write the missing words on the lines below.

1. The boy did not _____ the _____ the vendor put on his hot dog.

2. Although she was not a _____ character, her _____ sauce made her rudeness bearable.

3. Although it was tempting to _____ on the desserts, a fly in the custard made the meal rise in her _____ .

4. The disturbing story in the _____ of the week's news articles made it difficult for him to _____ his dinner.

5. I will _____ the soup with hot pepper flakes, even if summer is not really the _____ for a spicy dish.

6. After he _____ the eggs into soft peaks, he _____ the dirty dishes into the sink.

Please Define

Samuel Butler once said, "A definition is the enclosing of a wilderness of idea within a wall of words." Write your explanation of definition below.

_____

_____

Now write definitions for the following three words.

1. vexing _____

_____

2. superfluous _____

_____

3. preamble _____

_____

2

Believe It or Not

Create phony but believable definitions for the following words. How believable can you be? Share your definitions with classmates. Vote on the most believable definition for each word.

repugnant _____

_____

insomniac _____

_____

spectacles _____

_____

3

Compound Creation

Compound words can be strung together like dominoes to create a compound string.

Example: housework workout outside sidewalk walkway

Create your own compound string of at least six words.

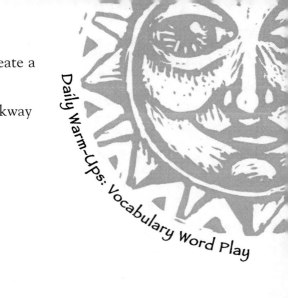

4

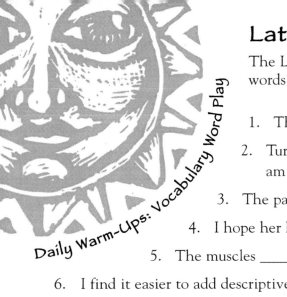

Latin Lingo

The Latin root *tract* means "to pull." Complete the sentences with words made with the root *tract*.

1. The _____ pulled the plow through the field.

2. Turn off the radio! I don't want any _____ while I am studying.

3. The paper _____ the story that was a hoax.

4. I hope her harsh voice will not _____ from the play.

5. The muscles _____ violently during a spasm.

6. I find it easier to add descriptive words to an essay than to _____ them.

7. The boy's leg was put in _____ to help it heal straight.

8. Although he was a reasonable person, he was _____ in matters of discipline.

9. The dentist needed strong pliers to _____ the molar.

10. I hope this case will not be a long, _____ battle.

Why Whirligig?

Write a silly paragraph that explains why a whirligig is called a whirligig.

6

Mystery Season

Think about words related to a season, such as summer or winter. Write a paragraph related to that season without using the name of the season. Exchange papers with a classmate. Can he or she guess what the season is?

7

Sci-fi Set

Imagine that you are a production assistant on a science fiction movie. Write a list of the materials you would expect to find on the set: the props, scenery, buildings, characters, and so forth. Feel free to create new words to describe what you need for the movie.

8

Veg Out

Name as many vegetables as you can that have three or more syllables.

I've Heard It Before

A **cliché** is an overused phrase or expression. For example, "food for thought" is a cliché that is no longer fresh. Make a list of as many clichés as possible in five minutes. Write them below.

10

Counting Clichés

Write a short paragraph using at least five clichés.

Hunting for Homophones

How many animal homophones can you think of? Here's an example: *moose* and *mousse*. Write three other examples below.

12

Vocabulary Lesson

Using a dictionary, find five unusual or difficult words. Write the definitions, then "teach" them to a partner. After you have taught the words, ask your partner to use each in a sentence. Did you both learn the meaning of the words? Write a reflection of the experience below.

13

Incredible Journey

The word *safari* is the Swahili word for *journey*. How many words can you think of for *journey*? Write a short paragraph about a journey you took. The journey could be to a faraway destination, or it could be a journey within. Use at least three synonyms for *journey* in your paragraph.

14

Be Happy

Imagine that you are writing a character sketch about a very happy person. Write ten words below that could be used to describe this person.

15

Animal Idioms

An **idiom** is a phrase that has come to have a meaning beyond
(and often quite different from) its literal definition. Many idioms
feature animals. Fill in each space below with an appropriate
animal idiom.

1. These nifty night clothes are _____.

2. It's _____ out! Dry off the puppy when
    you let it in.

3. Going with a group of friends to a movie is one thing; going to a frat party
    with a twenty-two-year-old is a _____.

4. Why are you so quiet today? Has the _____?

Now write two animal idioms of your own and include a meaning for each.

5. _____

6. _____

16

Be Positive

A **connotation** is an idea suggested by a word. Look at the pairs of words below. Match each positive word in the column on the left with a negative synonym on the right. Write the correct letter on the line.

____	1. save	a.	delusion
____	2. critical	b.	conceited
____	3. belief	c.	hoard
____	4. avenge	d.	carping
____	5. husky	e.	obese
____	6. confident	f.	retaliate

17

Red Alert

English is a language rich in adjectives. In the word search below, circle fourteen synonyms for the adjective *red*. You may want to brainstorm a list of synonyms to look for first.

```
E S T L O R E I C R A N I A R
F L E R G A R N E T I D L O A
R U N S E T T A I R B D N S B
O L I E T E L R A C S N O A A
S U M E B R E T T U S O S N N
V E R M I L L I O N T A M I N
I R A O B I G N F L O R I D I
P H C C T L I T S E M O R N C
U O M S E U Y Z R L M N C E Y
C N O I G T A R U B Y C U D E
E G D N U C T I O U S N D E X
C L A S F E D E F K O U J B A
K S E L E T E S S U R P M G B
S M A G E N T A I F J E K O F
I H F V A D E U N Q M C U L E
```

18

So Precise

When writing, it is important to use the most precise word to fit the meaning of a sentence. This makes your writing more interesting. For each pair of words below, circle the higher-degree word. Then write a sentence for each circled word.

1. torrent   shower

2. dainty   finicky

3. peril   danger

4. stubborn   obstinate

5. ornate   elegant

6. _____

7. _____

8. _____

9. _____

10. _____

19

© 2006 Walch Publishing

A World of Color

Next to each word below, write the color the word is associated with. If you need help, use a dictionary.

1. cyanotic _____

2. roseola _____

3. jaundice _____

4. azure _____

5. verdant _____

6. sanguine _____

7. blanch _____

8. grisaille _____

9. brunette _____

10. melatonin _____

20

© 2006 Walch Publishing

To a Degree

When writing, it is important to use the most precise word to fit the meaning of a sentence. This makes your writing more interesting. For each pair of words below, circle the lower-degree word. Then write a sentence for each circled word.

1. cool   frigid

2. forlorn   lonely

3. laudation   admiration

4. display   flaunt

5. clean   immaculate

6. _____

7. _____

8. _____

9. _____

10. _____

21

It's Elemental

Write each word under the appropriate element: earth, air, fire, or water.

aerosol   condensation   ignite   pulmonary

aquatic   ethereal   incendiary   pumice

char   geology   inflammable   respiration

clod   glacial   lachrymose   terrestrial

combustion   humidity   perspiration   territory

EARTH   AIR   FIRE   WATER

22

Decisions, Decisions

For each sentence, circle the correct word. Then on the line below, write the correct word's letter as indicated by the number in parentheses after the sentence. If you are correct for each sentence, the letters will spell two words that describe this activity.

1. I did not do very (good, well) on my geometry test. (1)

2. After the hurricane, we had to assess the (amount, number) of damage to the town. (3)

3. Please do not (hoard, horde) all the candy! (4)

4. The restaurant server was (disinterested, uninterested) in our complaints. (12)

5. I was not (conscience, conscious) for hours after the accident. (8)

6. How did you (loose, lose) the keys to the car? (3)

7. Aunt Bessie divided the pizza (among, between) the six players. (1)

8. That DVD player has many (good, well) features. (1)

9. The speaker is an (eminent, imminent) theologian. (5)

10. The words that describe this activity:

___ ___ ___ ___ ___   ___ ___ ___ ___

23

Character Traits

Listed below are words that writers use to describe characters. If the word has a positive connotation, write **P** next to it. If the word has a negative connotation, write **N** next to it.

_____ 1. arrogant

_____ 2. discreet

_____ 3. assertive

_____ 4. acerbic

_____ 5. confident

_____ 6. callous

_____ 7. impudent

_____ 8. misguided

_____ 9. benevolent

_____ 10. credulous

_____ 11. brutish

_____ 12. civil

_____ 13. credible

_____ 14. gallant

_____ 15. deceptive

_____ 16. congenial

_____ 17. aggressive

_____ 18. brash

24

Sky High

Think about what you see in the sky. Write the heavenly body related to each word below.

1. astral _____

2. stellar _____

3. lunar _____

4. solar _____

5. mercurial _____

Now brainstorm other words related to objects in outer space. Write them below.

25

Body and Soul

The word *psychology* is derived from the Greek root *psyche*, which means "soul." Write other words that begin with *psych*.

26

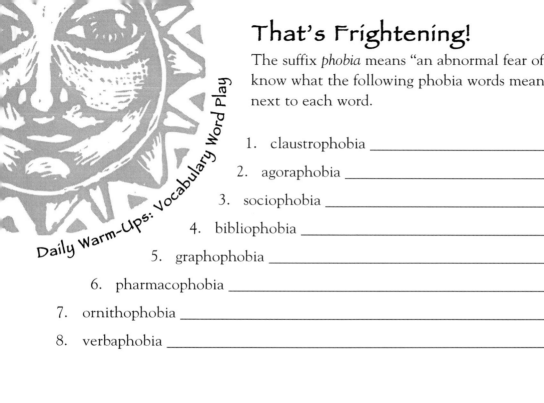

That's Frightening!

The suffix *phobia* means "an abnormal fear of something." Do you know what the following phobia words mean? Write the definition next to each word.

1. claustrophobia _____

2. agoraphobia _____

3. sociophobia _____

4. bibliophobia _____

5. graphophobia _____

6. pharmacophobia _____

7. ornithophobia _____

8. verbaphobia _____

27

Weather Alert

You are asked to write copy for a weather broadcast. Choose the word from the box that best completes each sentence.

contiguous	dissipate	stagnate
depression	saturate	turbulence

1. This forecast is for the forty-eight _____ states.

2. In the Northeast, a cold front will _____ over the area.

3. In the South, a tropical _____ is forming off the coast.

4. For those flying today, expect some _____ caused by severe winds.

5. The severe wind gusts are expected to _____ this afternoon.

6. You can expect heavy rain to _____ the ground.

Write two sentences using other words you hear in weather broadcasts.

7. _____

8. _____

28

© 2006 Walch Publishing

Let's Eat!

Match each of the following food words on the left with its clue on the right. Write the correct letter on the line.

___ 1. a pig

___ 2. someone who eats meat

___ 3. very juicy

___ 4. starving; very hungry

___ 5. relating to someone who has fine tastes

___ 6. something added to food

___ 7. without much taste

___ 8. extremely thin

a. bland

b. glutton

c. emaciated

d. carnivore

e. succulent

f. garnish

g. ravenous

h. epicurean

29

Rhyme Time

Rhyming is a form of word play even young children enjoy. See if you can make two-word rhymes based on the clues below.

1. an absorbent leg exercise
2. a mistake in the rain forest
3. a bee-bitten breathing organ
4. friend to do homework with
5. a pal in a novel

6. a sugary snack
7. a cool movie
8. a library burglar
9. a sparkly crown
10. a midnight meeting

30

Write two clues of your own and see if classmates can figure out your rhymes.

11. _____

12. _____

Animal Magnetism

The words on the left are related to certain animals. Match each word with the animal it refers to. Write the correct letter on the line.

____ 1.	bovine	a.	bee
____ 2.	canine	b.	bird
____ 3.	feline	c.	cat
____ 4.	ovine	d.	cow
____ 5.	porcine	e.	dog
____ 6.	equine	f.	fish
____ 7.	apiarian	g.	horse
____ 8.	avian	h.	ape
____ 9.	simian	i.	pig
____10.	piscine	j.	sheep

31

Animal Attributes

People give certain attributes to animals. For example, you may have heard the expression "as wise as an owl." For each attribute, write an animal that you associate with it. Answers may differ depending on cultural background.

1. cleverness _____

2. curiosity _____

3. loyalty _____

   4. stubbornness _____

      5. pride _____

         6. docility _____

            7. filthiness _____

               8. gentleness _____

                  9. luck _____

            10. deceitfulness _____

32

Sales Pitch

Advertisers want their audience to buy a product. To lure customers, some ads make larger-than-life claims. Imagine that you are an advertising copywriter for the following products. Describe each product using outsized adjectives. For example, a tasty new cookie might be described as a stupendous snack experience. Be sure to use at least one exaggerated adjective in each description.

1. a new sport utility vehicle

   _____

2. a line of sunglasses

   _____

3. a line of sneakers

   _____

4. a new video game

   _____

5. a new soft drink

   _____

33

Extreme Expressions

People use a variety of interesting words to describe something that is extreme or surprising. For example, have you ever heard someone tell a *whopper*, or an unbelievable story? Make a list of words that someone might use to describe something that goes beyond the run-of-the-mill.

34

"A" Crossword

Use the clues below to complete the crossword puzzle with words beginning with the letter *a*.

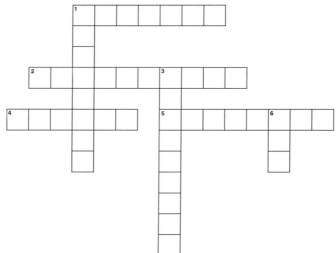

Across

1. severe in appearance

2. old-fashioned

4. smart

5. an object from a particular period, made by humans

Down

1. difficult to understand

3. showing lack of interest

6. appropriate

35

Interesting Idioms

Idioms are phrases or groups of words that are peculiar to a group of people. Write the meaning of each common idiom below.

1. hit the road _____

2. pull strings _____

3. come clean _____

4. blow a fuse _____

5. catch someone's eye _____

36

Now write two more idioms and their meanings.

6. _____

_____

7. _____

_____

© 2006 Walch Publishing

A Contradiction in Terms

An **oxymoron** is a pair of two terms that seemingly have opposite meanings. Look at the oxymorons below. Then add five of your own to the list.

black light

original copy

random order

jumbo shrimp

controlled chaos

pretty ugly

37

How Appealing!

See how many synonyms you can find for the word *appeal* in the
word search below. There are eight.

```
M K Z M X S U Y R O R E O E Y
D V P P U A S L X O C O T S U
H I T K I Z S E U N L P T E B
G K M P P A F Z R R Z S Q P D
B Q Y F L N A F T D B E H Y X
U Y V I V D Q P C F D F C E T
R O I N V O K E P Y Y A E S K
G X G H T U W P P L H Z E U T
E D C T A E R T N E Y U S S H
W D G H K W E Y H Y Q E E C D
O B W B M J W Q J E K Z B V K
N Z W L L R Z X R S Z U K S S
P F Q B G G V W A Y D J R N T
X J W Q S X R S B A J J D R D
H D U M C F K C I R G X H W A
```

38

Just the Opposite

Write as many antonyms as you can for the word *renounce*.

Palindrome Puzzler 1

Palindromes are words that read the same forward or backward. Here are three examples:

mom   radar   noon

How many can you think of? Write them below.

What's in a Name?

An **eponym** is a word based on a person—real or imagined—from whom something takes its name. Here are three examples:

diesel   Fahrenheit   napoleon

Now write five other examples of eponyms below.

41

Hunting Homographs

Homographs are words that have the same spelling but different meanings. Read the pairs of definitions below, and write the correct homograph on the line.

1. type of shoe; a cross between a donkey and a horse _____

2. strong desire; unit of money _____

3. to throw; a cut of beef _____

4. to jump over; a place for valuables _____

42

Now name three more homographs below.

The Same, But Different

A **heteronym** is a kind of homograph. It has the same spelling as another word, but it has a different meaning and a different pronunciation. Read the pairs of definitions below, and write the correct heteronym on the line.

1. satisfied; what's inside   _____

2. a thing; to protest   _____

3. very familiar; to suggest   _____

4. to say no; waste   _____

Now name three other heteronyms below.

43

Inner Conflict

A **contronym** is a word that has meanings that contradict each other. For example, you may receive a citation for your outstanding service, or you may get a citation for speeding. A citation can mean an acknowledgment of a good deed, or disapproval of bad behavior.

Read the pairs of definitions below, and write the correct contronym on each line.

44

1. to cling tightly; to cut apart   _____

2. support for an action; penalty for an action   _____

3. moving quickly; unable to move at all   _____

4. close attention, supervision; an error caused by inattentiveness   _____

What Nonsense!

Have you ever forgotten the name of an object and substituted a nonsense word for it? For example, you might say *thingy* or *widget* if you can't remember the specific name for a device.

List as many nonsense words as you can that people use in place of specific names.

45

Big Time

There are many words in English that mean "big." In the word search below, circle thirteen synonyms for *big*.

```
H R S M O N U M E N T A L E C
E U Q U U R P B A I W V S N O
V I M W O M H U P A U N B I L
I D Y O Q M T U T L E J S T O
S S N M N N R G G M Q P Z N S
S U T J A G I O M E Q H G A S
A F K G K G O I N U W P N H A
M L R D A N O U R E L T G P L
Y A W N A N N G S D P I U E Q
G U T M A M M O T H C V R L Q
C I L K P D X O U T M A K E P
C U L R Q Z Y Y P J R S S T P
X I I A M Q R I O I X T E B F
O S U O R E N E G K U W A Z N
O M Y P L U T K S C Q R O A N
```

46

Plural Power

Below are the singular forms of some tricky words. Write the plural form of each word on the line.

1. activity   _____

2. video   _____

3. tooth   _____

4. loaf   _____

5. hero   _____

6. woman   _____

7. ox   _____

8. goose   _____

9. medium   _____

10. basis   _____

11. family   _____

12. turkey   _____

13. waltz   _____

47

How Beautiful!

Imagine the most beautiful scene you have ever witnessed. Write fifteen words you would use to describe this beautiful scene.

48

Fear Factor

Be creative and think of a new phobia. It may be a fear you have; for example, perhaps you have a fear of cell phones. Create a new phobia word to describe your fear, such as *cellphonobia*.

Describe your phobia, and write its name below.

49

Adjective Challenge

Make a list of your ten favorite adjectives. Then write a paragraph using those adjectives.

50

The Long and Short of It

Do you have a nickname? Lots of people do. And lots of words have shortened forms as well. Write the complete word for each clipped word below.

1. plane _____

2. gator _____

3. hose _____

4. ump _____

5. copter _____

6. memo _____

7. fridge _____

8. chimp _____

51

Just a Tad

How many ways do you know of to say "a very small amount"?
In the word search below, circle ten words with that meaning.

```
L D L G C N M H D D J D N U O
E L C I T R A P N A T O I Z Y
X G U X E K N R H K S W T M N
N C Y H C C U E C W N H R W S
J E N I Z L V E G C X X W C S
C L G N C R P T K D K M I K D
R K M T L S N Z M Q I N S R S
Y P W Y D R E Y N J T M A P K
E M V R B A W S S I D M S S W
C J A T T V R L F Z M T G P
A W J J O E Z L C Y P C R N F
R R E R A P A R T M O V H C F
T P Y H J I J M R G R A I N Y
I R J L F V K V V A V W G K D
P Z R M T N P J J Z C E D E G
```

52

Daily Warm-Ups: Vocabulary Word Play

Let There Be Light

The words in this crossword puzzle all relate to light. Solve the puzzle using the clues below.

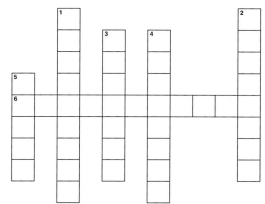

Across

6. a wavelength beyond visible light

Down

1. the flash of light produced by the discharge of atmospheric electricity

2. the colors that make up white light, arranged by wavelength

3. a skin pigment that helps protect against sunlight

4. glowing

5. the opening in the eye that responds to light

53

© 2006 Walch Publishing

Shakespeare Stumper

William Shakespeare added thousands of new words to the English language. Read the clues below. Then choose the word from the box that best matches each clue. Write it on the line.

courtship	excellent	laughable	obscene
dwindle	gloomy	lonely	premeditated

_____ 1. ridiculous

_____ 2. the act of dating

_____ 3. dark

_____ 4. repulsive

_____ 5. solitary

_____ 6. to decrease

_____ 7. superior

_____ 8. deliberate

54

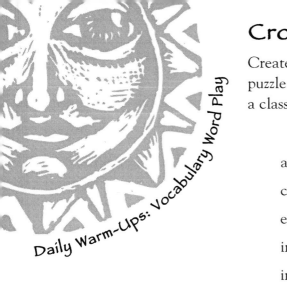

Crossword Challenge

Create a crossword puzzle with the words listed below. Draw your puzzle and write the clues on a separate sheet of paper. Then have a classmate complete the puzzle.

acquiesce

capitulate

eschew

inculcate

indomitable

pernicious

pervasive

tenacity

55

Part of the Whole

Read the definitions below. Each one refers to a word part. Write the word part and an example of a word that uses it.

1. light ◯ ___ ___ ___ ___   Example: _____

2. across ___ ◯ ___ ___ ___   Example: _____

3. half ___ ◯ ___ ___   Example: _____

4. small ___ ___ ◯ ___ ___   Example: _____

5. among, between ___ ___ ___ ◯ ___   Example: _____

6. false ___ ___ ___ ___ ◯ ___   Example: _____

7. too little ___ ___ ___ ◯ ___   Example: _____

8. above ◯ ___ ___ ___ ___   Example: _____

56

Now write the circled letters in order to answer the following question: Where does a prefix go?

It _____ a word.

Singular Sensation

Below are the plural forms of some tricky words. Write the singular form of each word on the line.

1. bacteria _____

2. cherub _____

3. data _____

4. crises _____

5. wolves _____

6. sheep _____

7. beaux _____

8. criteria _____

9. phenomena _____

10. sons-in-law _____

57

Sneaky Synonyms

Each word below contains letters in order that form a synonym of the word. Write each synonym on the line.

1. fallacies _____

2. blossom _____

3. gigantic _____

4. hatred _____

5. separate _____

6. slithered _____

7. masculine _____

58

Now think of two other words that each have a synonym contained within the word. Write them below.

Synonym Brainstorm

Finding synonyms for words can be fun. For the two words listed below, think of as many synonyms as you can. Write the synonyms below each word.

walk   courage

It's About Time!

The words in this crossword puzzle all have to do with time. Solve the puzzle using the clues below.

Across

1. before birth
3. a long time ago (before the biblical flood)
4. before a wedding
5. at the same time

Down

1. after death
2. before the American Civil War

Just a Tiny Bit

There are many degrees of smallness. Circle ten synonyms for *small* in the word search below. You may want to brainstorm a list of synonyms first.

```
I M E V I T U N I M I D K H F
E N J A A E E Q O I J M W C X
R G F F U T L P M C C U E Q G
U K F I I O G U D R V K E U L
T P Q T N W B D C O F T W I L
A M E U N I P V J S Y X L I Z
I P D N E N T R S C U L N A S
N M I N U T E E A O I N N R E
I X N X Y P R X S P R E I P J
M S W L L B P E U I T X X M A
D F Y I Q V O T A C M P P G L
A U H R S U I J O U T A U W Z
A X K V I A P V L J E E L N G
F T G B N I J V Z P M W G C Y
K G V L K J L A S O W B Y Z K
```

61

Palindrome Puzzler II

Palindromes are words that read the same forward or backward.
Write the correct palindrome next to each clue below.

1. protective cloth _____

2. something put in mouth _____

3. pertaining to a citizen _____

4. a type of canoe _____

5. an exclamation _____

6. father _____

7. detection system _____

8. past tense of *do* _____

62

Oxymoron Matchup

An oxymoron is a pair of two terms that seemingly have opposite meanings. Match each word on the left with a word on the right to form an oxymoron. Write the correct letter on the line.

___ 1. freezer   a. familiar

___ 2. somewhat   b. grief

___ 3. guest   c. burn

___ 4. definite   d. dressed

___ 5. strangely   e. host

___ 6. good   f. maybe

___ 7. barely   g. lethal

63

© 2006 Walch Publishing

Eight Is Enough

The prefix *oct* or *octo* refers to the number eight. Complete the crossword puzzle with words beginning with the prefix *oct* or *octo*.

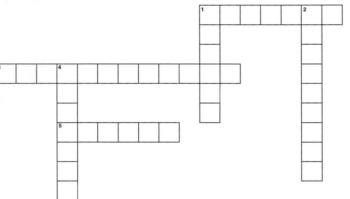

Across

1. a plane figure with eight sides

3. a person who is between the ages of eighty and ninety

5. a chemical in petroleum

Down

1. a series of eight notes

2. a line of verse containing eight metrical feet

4. a mollusk with eight arms

"O" Puzzler

Create a short crossword puzzle using the words below beginning with the letter *o*. Draw your puzzle and write the clues on a separate sheet of paper. Then have a classmate complete the puzzle.

obtrusive

obviate

omnipotent

opprobrious

oracle

ostensible

65

Larger Than Life

Some adjectives describe things that are larger than life or far beyond the ordinary. Circle ten such adjectives in the word search below.

```
D T S O R M M I K S I T V S Q
V A H U D A T J G N N P G U H
O V J T O Y X C D A A D F O R
B F S Y E I Q B G V B W T I S
H B L F B X T A Q E F M S T L
S X N A U X V A H R Z R F N U
U R W R M A O P T P J A U E X
L E X O R B I T A N T H O T U
P N Z T U U O T L D E P T E R
B I X Q E M A Y R Y U T O R I
A E H S I V A L A L G S S P A
G E M D S S F E E N E X F O N
T X T A Q N A N U T T Q N B T
A Y Q A R R T M R I W K I J H
Z O U Q K G H Q D E Q W Z D D
```

66

Daily Warm-Ups: Vocabulary Word Play

Crossword Conundrum 1

The words in this crossword puzzle are all synonyms and antonyms for words that begin with the letter *a*. Solve the puzzle using the clues. You may use a thesaurus if needed.

Across

4. an antonym of *alleviate*
7. a synonym of *alleviate*
8. an antonym of *anodyne*

Down

1. a synonym of *avid*
2. an antonym of *apex*

3. a synonym of *apex*
5. a synonym of *anodyne*
6. an antonym of *avid*

© 2006 Walch Publishing

Roots of Science

Look at the scientific roots and their meanings below. Write an example word using each root to complete the chart.

Root	Meaning	Example
1. bronch	windpipe	
2. gastro	relating to the stomach	
3. chemo	drug	
4. hemo	blood	
5. archae	ancient	
6. micro	small	

Daily Warm-Ups: Vocabulary Word Play

68

Sad Synonyms

The word *sad* is overused and tends to make your writing dull. How many other words can you think of that mean "sad"? Write them below. Then use two of the words in sentences.

69

Something in Common

What do the following words have in common? Write your answer below.

bagpipe

balalaika

harpsichord

ocarina

pennywhistle

piccolo

tympani

zither

70

Crossword Conundrum 11

The words in this crossword puzzle are all synonyms and antonyms for words that begin with the letter *b*. Solve the puzzle using the clues. You may use a thesaurus if needed.

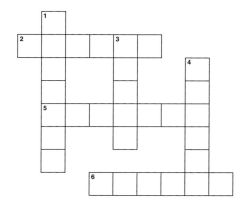

Across

2. an antonym of *blatant*

5. a synonym of *blatant*

6. an antonym of *buttress*

Down

1. a synonym of *buttress*

3. an antonym of *berserk*

4. a synonym of *berserk*

71

The Write Stuff

The root *script* means "write." List as many words containing this root as possible.

72

He Said, She Said

When writers create dialogue for their characters, they often substitute more colorful verbs for the word *said*. List several verbs that a writer might use that could be substituted for *said*.

73

Crazy English

Richard Lederer is the author of a book called *Crazy English*. He likes to have fun with words. Here are some interesting comments about words in the English language. Can you think of others? Write your ideas below.

Why is there no egg in eggplant?

A guinea pig is not a pig.

Fireflies are actually beetles.

74

SAT Review

Write an antonym for each of these commonly used SAT words.

1. equitable _____

2. benevolent _____

3. advent _____

4. reclusive _____

5. ephemeral _____

6. haggard _____

7. oblivious _____

8. Lilliputian _____

75

Crossword Conundrum III

The words in this crossword puzzle are all synonyms and antonyms for words that begin with the letter *c*. Solve the puzzle using the clues. You may use a thesaurus if needed.

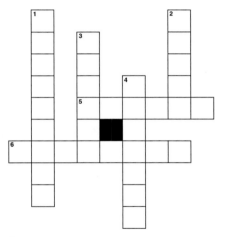

76

Across

5. a synonym of *cowardly*
6. a synonym of *careless*

Down

1. an antonym of *calm*
2. an antonym of *cowardly*
3. a synonym of *calm*
4. an antonym of *careless*

SAT Synonyms

Write a synonym for each of these commonly used SAT words.

1. prevarication _____

2. futile _____

3. indigent _____

4. somnolent _____

5. tenacity _____

6. draconian _____

7. trepidation _____

8. elixir _____

77

The Right Choice

Choose the word that best fits the definition below.

a light umbrella that protects you from the sun

    a.   croupier

    b.   parasol

    c.   persimmon

Now use each answer choice above in a sentence of your own.

78

Please Define

What is the meaning of the word *picayune*?

a. shaky; run-down

b. harsh; unpleasant

c. petty; trivial

Now use *picayune* in a sentence of your own.

79

Choose Wisely

Choose the word that best fits the definition below.

a fit of rage or hysteria

    a. constellation

    b. colloquialism

    c. conniption

Now use each answer choice above in a sentence of your own.

80

Crossword Conundrum IV

The words in this crossword puzzle are all synonyms and antonyms for words that begin with the letter *d*. Solve the puzzle using the clues. You may use a thesaurus if needed.

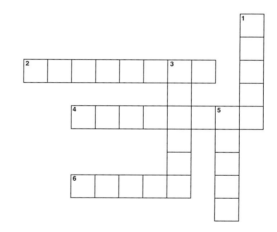

Across

2. an antonym of *diffuse*

4. an antonym of *dissuade*

6. a synonym of *diffuse*

Down

1. a synonym of *dexterous*

3. an antonym of *dexterous*

5. a synonym of *dissuade*

81

© 2006 Walch Publishing

How Insulting!

At one time, one of the worst insults was to question someone's honor. In the word search below, circle ten insulting names a gentleman might have called someone of questionable character.

```
Q W F L E J Q P V K Z J D S I
T Z N I U A E F W Z D X F V E
L Y E W M W G C L B T U O L U
J J H G R N N X N C Y V L N I
Z B D N F O Y Q Q I N M T G A
K X A H O I X D R Q L R D W V
W O C F F L D X A T C R D D I
U H G P M L V B D E A A T G O
G V N F D A C H A U U K X V K
R T I N F C V X G Z J D B U O
K O Y L R S L K B O U N D E R
N D O O L P C A I K H U O H C
A D G B L A B V R A S U I V T
V U P F L R I U J P V P H Z K
E T K B B L C N K N T E U P B
```

82

In Good Shape

What is the shape of the Washington Monument?

a. quadrangle

b. pentagon

c. obelisk

Now use each answer choice above in a sentence of your own.

83

A Common Thread

What do these words have in common? Write your ideas below.

cappuccino

cayenne

falafel

kohlrabi

molasses

nougat

rutabaga

succotash

Now use two of the words above in sentences of your own.

84

How Redundant!

A **tautology** is a needless repetition of words or ideas. For example, the phrase *widow woman* is redundant. Yogi Berra was famous for using tautology with statements such as the following: "You can observe a lot just by watching."

Can you think of other tautologies? Write them below.

85

Blue Hues

There are many different shades of blue. Circle ten words that describe the blue hue in the word search below.

```
S  J  E  D  H  E  M  G  U  B  D  A  S  V  I
I  N  D  I  G  O  A  X  Z  O  B  M  E  E  E
L  F  S  T  E  S  R  I  T  T  I  Q  S  R  Q
Y  Q  L  K  T  J  I  C  Z  I  V  H  I  Z  B
E  T  J  K  W  G  N  O  A  A  S  H  O  C  C
L  L  O  H  P  C  E  J  S  U  P  W  U  W  M
C  G  K  V  K  C  C  Q  J  P  Q  F  Q  A  H
Y  O  E  N  P  M  F  X  A  H  I  A  R  G  G
K  Y  B  H  I  L  W  S  G  V  E  R  U  Z  A
S  J  P  A  A  W  N  X  Q  S  O  Z  T  H  H
M  N  W  P  L  G  I  U  I  T  Z  R  Q  Z  W
F  N  I  H  M  T  I  R  H  L  Y  S  Z  E  J
L  S  Q  O  L  B  T  S  E  D  F  I  Y  I  A
F  S  H  W  T  C  D  F  C  P  E  A  Q  E  H
U  E  H  X  G  G  V  I  L  Q  Z  Y  E  S  I
```

86

Crossword Conundrum V

The words in this crossword puzzle are all synonyms and antonyms for words that begin with the letter *f*. Solve the puzzle using the clues. You may use a thesaurus if needed.

Across

1. an antonym of *fierce*
3. a synonym of *fierce*
6. an antonym of *failure*

Down

2. a synonym of *failure*
4. an antonym of *feeble*
5. a synonym of *feeble*

Prefix Power

For each word below, choose a prefix from the box that makes the word negative. Then use the word in a sentence.

| dis- | il- | im- | ir- | non- | un- |

1. porous _____

2. pertinent _____

3. relevant _____

4. content _____

5. guarded _____

6. legible _____

88

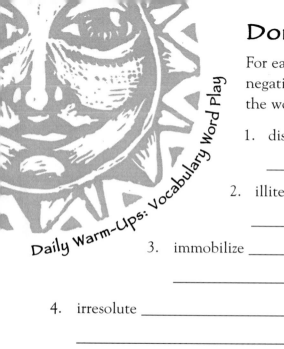

Don't Be Negative

For each word below, remove the prefix that makes the word negative. Then write a sentence using the positive form of the word.

1. discharge _____

_____

2. illiterate _____

_____

3. immobilize _____

_____

4. irresolute _____

_____

5. nonfiction _____

_____

6. infertile _____

_____

89

Spelling Bee

Read each word below. If the word is spelled correctly, write **correct** on the line. If it is spelled incorrectly, write the correct spelling of the word.

Word	Correct Spelling
1. papparazi	_____
2. cacaphony	_____
3. tourniquet	_____
4. discumbolulate	_____
5. epigram	_____
6. abundent	_____
7. entraprener	_____
8. merangue	_____

90

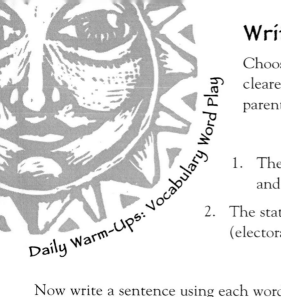

Writing Workshop

Choosing precise words when writing makes your work much clearer. Read the following sentences. Circle the word in parentheses that best completes each sentence.

1. The medical student's (indentation, incision, gash) was clear and precise.

2. The state senator promised to pay more attention to the needs of the (electorates, legislators, constituents) who voted her into office.

Now write a sentence using each word choice above that you did not use to complete a sentence.

91

Crossword Conundrum VI

The words in this crossword puzzle are all synonyms and antonyms for words that begin with the letter *g*. Solve the puzzle using the clues. You may use a thesaurus if needed.

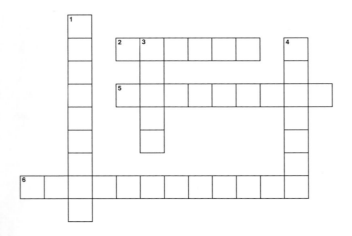

92

Across

2. an antonym of *gradual*

5. an antonym of *gallant*

6. an antonym of *glib*

Down

1. a synonym of *gradual*

3. a synonym of *gallant*

4. a synonym of *glib*

Getting Stronger

Each continuum below shows words listed in order of strength. On the blank lines under each continuum, write words that fit appropriately. One continuum has been done for you.

microscopic   small   big   gargantuan

1.

    slow   quick

_____   _____

2.

effortless   challenging

_____   _____

3.

inadequate   excessive

_____   _____

93

Word Find

Insupportable means "intolerable," or something that you just can't stand. How many words can you form from the letters of the word *insupportable*? Write as many as you can. Then compare your list with those of classmates.

INSUPPORTABLE

94

Playing Favorites

Think about your favorite words—words that you find yourself using a lot. Make a list of these words. Think about why they appeal to you. Then write your reasons below.

95

Defined by Example

Editor and debunker H. L. Mencken once wrote, "A cynic is a man who, when he smells flowers, looks around for a coffin." Here, the word *cynic* is defined by an example.

Choose one of the people below who you might find at your school. Write a descriptive definition for this person like Mencken's.

a driver's ed teacher

a volleyball player

a drummer

a poet

a driven student

a slacker

a strict teacher

96

The Power of Words

Ingrid Bengis, a writer and teacher, once said, "For me, words are a form of action, capable of influencing change." Do you agree? Explain below.

97

Artful Alliteration

Alliteration is the repetition of sounds in a series, especially initial sounds. The phrase *soft serenade* is an example of alliteration.

Make an alliterative phrase using each word below.

1. hair _____

2. sunshine _____

3. moonlight _____

4. bus _____

5. monkey _____

6. apartment _____

7. pavement _____

8. chalkboard _____

98

How Absurd!

The following sentences all contain misplaced modifiers. In the space below, draw a cartoon showing the absurdity of one of the sentences. Then rewrite the sentence to convey the meaning the author intended.

Do you have any problem talking with the cat yowling on the phone?

I smelled the flowers walking through the garden.

The dog ran after the boy chasing his tail.

The singer hit the high note gripping the microphone stand.

99

Commonly Confused

Here are some commonly confused words. Circle the correct word to answer each question below.

1. Which kind of remark hurts?   a. engaging   b. disparaging

2. Which is your job?   a. vocation   b. avocation

3. Which means that you are a beginner?   a. novena   b. novice

4. Which occurrence is worse?   a. calamity   b. catastrophe

5. Which is the top?   a. zenith   b. nadir

100

Now write two questions of your own using these pairs of words:

route/rout   indolent/idle

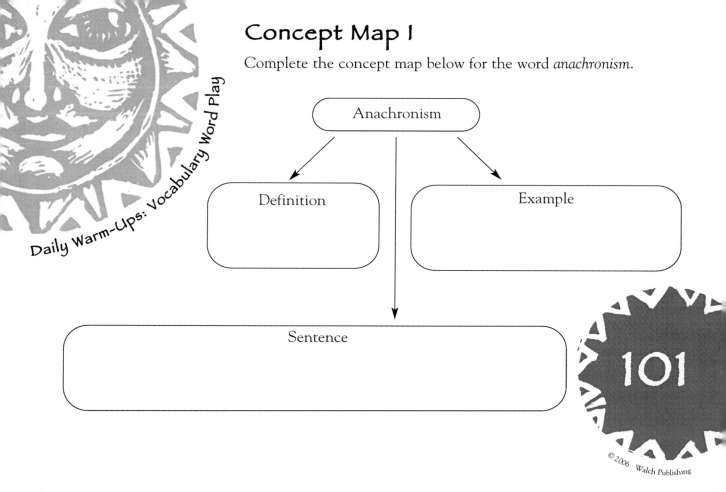

Concept Map I

Complete the concept map below for the word *anachronism*.

Anachronism

Definition

Example

Sentence

101

Concept Map 11

Complete the concept map below for the word *euphemism*.

```
                        ┌─────────────────────┐
                        │      Euphemism      │
                        └─────────────────────┘
                    ↙              │              ↘
   ┌──────────────────────┐       │       ┌──────────────────────┐
   │     Definition       │       │       │      Example         │
   │                      │       │       │                      │
   │                      │       │       │                      │
   └──────────────────────┘       │       └──────────────────────┘
                                   ↓
                 ┌──────────────────────────────────────┐
                 │              Sentence                 │
                 │                                       │
                 │                                       │
                 └──────────────────────────────────────┘
```

102

© 2006 Walch Publishing

Clever Crossword

Here's a crossword puzzle that uses all *-ing* clues. See if you can solve it. You may use a thesaurus if needed.

Across

2. walking

3. daunting

4. severing

7. startling

8. wandering

Down

1. fighting

5. demanding

6. avoiding

Critic's Corner I

Write a favorable review of a movie or a television show you have seen recently. Use at least six of the words below. If possible, use all of the words.

astute   genuine

cogent   laudable

compelling   mastery

forte   prowess

104

Critic's Corner II

Write an unfavorable review of a movie or a television show you have seen recently. Use at least six of the words below. If possible, use all of the words.

dearth	mundane
feckless	passable
forego	paucity
inferior	tedious

105

No Doubt About It

The word *doubt* comes from the Latin word *doubitare*, which means "to be of two minds." Below, write three things that you have doubts about and three things for which you have no doubt.

Doubts   **No Doubts**

How Poetic!

Write at least one word that rhymes with each word below.

1. liberty _____

2. brotherhood _____

3. equality _____

Now write a short poem using some of the rhyming words you brainstormed above.

107

© 2006 Walch Publishing

Be Inventive

Imagine an invention that you would find useful. Sketch your invention below. Then give it a descriptive name. Feel free to make up new words to describe and promote your invention.

108

So Bad It's Good

You may have heard of the Bulwer-Lytton Fiction Contest, in which entrants write the most clichéd opening sentence possible for a story. The classic example is the opening phrase *It was a dark and stormy night* to begin a mystery story.

For each genre of short story below, write a stereotypical opening sentence. Then write an opening sentence that might hook a reader.

a whodunit

_____

_____

a horror story

_____

_____

a sci-fi story

_____

_____

109

Broadway Spoof

Imagine that you are going to write a musical for Broadway that spoofs something you know about. An example of a spoof is the *Scary Movie* series, which incorporates the standard horror-movie situations in a comedy. Think of your concept, then write a catchy title for your show, using a pun or other word play.

110

The Squeaky Wheel

Write a short, imaginary letter of complaint. Instead of closing with *Sincerely* or *Cordially* or another typical closing, use a phrase that conveys your annoyance. An example is *In consternation*, John Doe.

Name Game

Some names really seem to fit their owners, such as Dr. Welby. Others seem to contradict their owners, such as Dr. Coff. For each profession below, think of either a fitting or a strikingly unsuitable name for a person who holds that job. Write your name on the line.

1. dentist _____

2. gym teacher _____

3. baker _____

4. waiter _____

5. computer programmer _____

6. writer _____

7. police officer _____

112

Foreign Phrase Matchup I

We use many foreign phrases in our conversations. Match each French phrase on the left with its English definition on the right. Write the correct letter on the line.

___ 1. faux pas

___ 2. raison d'être

___ 3. coup de grace

___ 4. piece de resistance

___ 5. idée fixe

___ 6. pas de deux

___ 7. joie de vivre

a. final blow

b. guiding purpose

c. intricate activity involving two parties

d. love of life

e. masterpiece

f. mistake

g. obsession

113

Foreign Phrase Matchup II

Latin phrases show up in English frequently. Match each Latin phrase on the left with its English definition on the right. Write the correct letter on the line. Then use one of the Latin phrases below in a sentence.

____ 1. ad hoc

____ 2. ad nauseam

____ 3. ad infinitum

____ 4. a priori

____ 5. ipso facto

____ 6. non sequitur

____ 7. status quo

____ 8. in flagrante delicto

a. as a consequence of a mere fact

b. based on assumption

c. endlessly; indefinitely

d. for this particular purpose

e. in the act of committing a crime

f. something that does not follow logically

g. the existing state of affairs

h. to the point of sickness

114

Deft Definitions

Doug Larson said, "If the English language made any sense, a catastrophe would be an apostrophe with fur." For each word below, write what someone who does not know the definition might think it is. Then write the real definition.

1. rebuttal

    _____   _____

2. contraband

    _____   _____

3. infraction

    _____   _____

4. mundane

    _____   _____

5. intangible

    _____   _____

115

Don't Dis Me!

The prefix *dis-* can mean "not," "opposite of," "off," or "away."
Match each word on the left with its definition on the right.
Write the correct letter on the line.

_____ 1. disparage

_____ 2. disdain

_____ 3. disbar

_____ 4. dismay

_____ 5. distill

_____ 6. distress

_____ 7. discriminate

_____ 8. dispute

_____ 9. distribute

a. to deprive of the right to practice law

b. to refine

c. to recognize a difference

d. to discredit

e. to reject

f. to quarrel

g. to divide

h. to be filled with apprehension

i. to cause misery

116

Everyday Language

The word *vernacular* means "everyday language." How many words can you make from the letters in the word *vernacular*? There are over 120! Write as many as you can in five minutes.

117

Take a Number

Read the sentences below. Complete each with a number-related word. Write the word on the line.

1. A _____ is a special kind of poem with five lines.

2. After middle school, one attends _____ school.

3. A _____ is an animal that has two feet.

4. When Kim is seventy years old, she'll be a _____.

5. A _____ is an arthropod; despite the name, most of these creatures do not have one hundred legs.

6. Decisions regarding national security are made at the _____.

7. My dad's _____ plants bloom every other year.

8. A police officer's _____ includes a blue suit and a gold badge.

9. My town is almost three hundred years old; soon, we'll celebrate its _____.

10. The _____ bill had support from both political parties.

118

Fashionable Descriptions

Fashion is all about the way things look. Fashion ads often use interesting words to describe things. Imagine that you are writing the copy for a fashion catalog. The theme is food, and all the ads have been photographed in restaurants, on farms, in orchards, or other places related to food. Describe the following items using food words. For example, a brown sweater might be described as a chocolate shrug or a chestnut cardigan.

1. a red skirt _____

2. a pair of blue trousers _____

3. a pair of green shorts _____

4. a black coat _____

5. a purple blazer _____

6. an orange blouse _____

7. a gray tie _____

119

Actions Speak Louder

Abigail Adams wrote in a letter to John Adams in 1774, "We have too many high-sounding words, and too few actions that correspond with them."

Think about the time when Abigail Adams lived. What kind of high-sounding words might have been used during the revolutionary period? What kind of high-minded actions might Mrs. Adams have wanted to see? Write two lists in the space below.

High-sounding words   **High-minded actions**

Daily Warm-Ups: Vocabulary Word Play

120

© 2006 Walch Publishing

Music's Message

Think about the lyrics to one of your favorite songs. What words are repeated most often? Why? Write your thoughts below.

121

The American Way

The phrases *star-spangled banner* and *stars and stripes* bring up strong images of the American flag. Think of a phrase that captures the image of each monument below.

1. the Statue of Liberty _____

2. Mount Rushmore _____

3. the Washington Monument _____

Now write a phrase that helps a reader picture a landmark in your own town or city.

122

Alphabet Trail

Fill in the alphabet trail with words that begin and end with the letters given. Follow the arrows when writing in the answers.

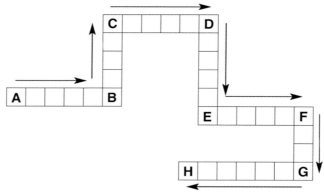

A: a word that may modify an adjective

B: fundamental

C: frank

D: to damage someone's reputation

E: to surround and cover

F: to whip

G: to decorate

On the Job

Surnames often refer to a profession. See if you can match each name on the left with the job it refers to on the right. Write the correct letter on the line.

___ 1. Carter   a. barrel maker

___ 2. Cooper   b. clothes maker

___ 3. Taylor   c. flour grinder

___ 4. Smith   d. metalworker

___ 5. Miller   e. transporter of goods

124

A Living Language

English is a living language. It grows and changes over time. Below is a list of obsolete words, or words that are no longer used. Write what you think each verb might mean.

1. crine _____

2. dwine _____

3. gowl _____

4. whingle _____

5. elden _____

125

Language of Origin

Many English words are derived, or come from, words in other languages. Some words are taken directly from another language and used commonly. See if you can match each word on the left with its language of origin on the right. Write the correct letter on the line.

___ 1. chagrin   a. French

___ 2. ersatz   b. Spanish

___ 3. vigilante   c. Italian

___ 4. kamikaze   d. German

___ 5. brio   e. Japanese

126

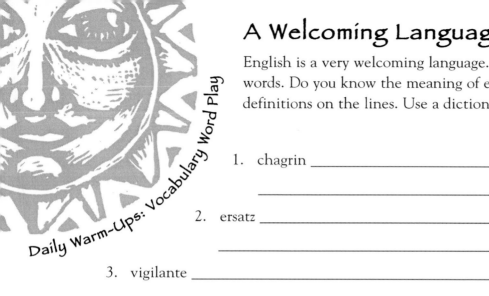

A Welcoming Language

English is a very welcoming language. It adopts many foreign words. Do you know the meaning of each word below? Write your definitions on the lines. Use a dictionary if needed.

1. chagrin _____

_____

2. ersatz _____

_____

3. vigilante _____

_____

4. kamikaze _____

_____

5. brio _____

_____

127

Obsolete Adjectives

English is a living language. It grows and changes over time. Below is a list of obsolete words, or words that are no longer used. On the lines below, write what you think each adjective might mean.

1. fluttersome _____

2. janglesome _____

3. lugsome _____

4. sweltersome _____

   5. tanglesome _____

128

The Meaning of a Name

Names can have specific meanings. For example, the name Rex means "king." What do you think the following names mean? Write your answers on the lines.

1. Felix _____

2. Quentin _____

3. Bailey _____

4. Bianca _____

5. Paige _____

129

A Different Dialogue

Below are some obsolete words and their definitions. Use at least three of the words in a short dialogue you might have at school. Use the words as though they are in common use today.

smeke: to flatter someone excessively (to kiss up)

forswunk: worn out from working

sloom: to sleep heavily

embranglement: puzzlement

drumble: one who does a thing without knowing how to do it

130

Artful Adjectives

Some words come from a person, real or imagined. For example, if someone describes the place where they work as Dickensian, you know it must be difficult and oppressive. This is how Charles Dickens showed work life in his books.

Think of a favorite author or character. Use that figure's name as an adjective. Write a sentence or two using the adjective.

131

Emotional Roller Coaster

People's emotions can change quickly, depending on what is happening. Imagine that you are writing about a character who is having mood swings. For each emotion below, write an emotion that would show a dramatic mood swing. For example, if someone is elated, a mood swing might have him or her feeling depressed.

1. apathetic _____

2. tranquil _____

3. winsome _____

4. euphoric _____

132

How Do You Feel?

Choose an emotion from the list below. Describe a situation in which you might feel that way.

anxious

disinterested

enraged

intrigued

obligated

133

Well-Known Monikers

Some people are so well known for something that their name becomes a noun to replace that thing. For example, if someone "needs your John Hancock," you know that person wants your signature. John Hancock was a famous signer of the Declaration of Independence.

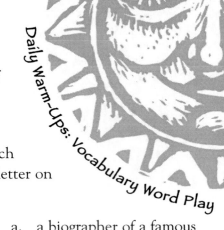

Can you guess which person's name has become which noun? Match each name on the left to the item on the right. Write the correct letter on the line.

134

____ 1. Shirley Temple, beloved child actress

____ 2. Mae West, voluptuous film star

____ 3. Benedict Arnold, American Revolution general who joined the British side

____ 4. (James) Boswell, writer who wrote about the life of Samuel Johnson

a. a biographer of a famous contemporary

b. a nonalcoholic drink

c. a traitor

d. an inflatable life vest

Days of Our Lives

The days of the week are named after gods of various cultures. Think about how you feel about each day of the week. Rename each day, incorporating the name of a real or a fictional character that shows how you feel.

135

Technologically Advanced

Technology has a strong influence on language. Make a list of as many e-mail and text-messaging abbreviations, emoticons, and terms as you can. Then compare your list with a partner's. Maybe you'll learn some new words!

136

A Popular Pastime

Sports are a popular pastime in the United States. People often use sports expressions in conversation. For example, the statement "Daniel really dropped the ball on Valentine's Day" means that Daniel really goofed.

Write at least three sentences using sports expressions. Do you think the general public would automatically know what each expression means? Or are some expressions very specific and only true fans would understand them? Write your thoughts below.

137

I Think I Can

Students spend a lot of time thinking. How many ways to say *think* can you think of? Circle ten synonyms for *think* in the word search below.

```
D C S Z O F R R F C V Q C V J
A E Z K N K E R O X I G L B R
Q R L C C D N G O K G X H Z M
U E B I N M I Q N P E D P T P
I B X O B T E Q W Z T S Y G Q
E R P I A E R T U X A L H C M
D A J T E R J A V X E B X N
B T E O F H Z A L N A X D B V
R E D I S N O C T N I L Z B T
L H Y B B T R M C E C M S R C
A E H N S O Y L M W M P U N E
C O N T E M P L A T E U L R L
V O W E I G H P Q W P Y S J F
F C C H Q O Z G A T K A Y E E
S W D O I S M Z X R D V G G R
```

138

Daily Warm-Ups: Vocabulary Word Play

Crossword Conundrum VII

The words in this crossword puzzle are all synonyms and antonyms for words that begin with the letter *h*. Solve the puzzle using the clues. You may use a thesaurus if needed.

Across

3. a synonym of *heinous*
6. an antonym of *hamper*

Down

1. a synonym of *hamper*
2. an antonym of *heinous*
4. an antonym of *haphazard*
5. a synonym of *haphazard*

139

© 2006 Walch Publishing

How Unpleasant!

A **euphemism** is a substitution of an agreeable expression for an unpleasant one. Match each blunt truth on the left with the euphemism on the right. Write the correct letter on the line.

___ 1. vomiting   a. in a family way

___ 2. pregnant   b. a correctional facility

___ 3. prison   c. losing your lunch

140

Kick the Bucket

A **euphemism** is a substitution of an agreeable expression for an unpleasant one. There are many euphemisms for death. See how many you can come up with in five minutes. List them below.

141

Opposites Attract

Read the words below. Circle the word that is most opposite of the word in capital letters.

1. DULL
   a. flat
   b. bright
   c. obscure

2. HONEST
   a. aboveboard
   b. realistic
   c. deceptive

3. AVENGE
   a. vindicate
   b. reciprocate
   c. forgive

4. ENDURANCE
   a. weakness
   b. persistence
   c. intolerance

5. HINDER
   a. obstruct
   b. impede
   c. assist

Now use each word listed above in capital letters in a sentence of your own.

142

Rebus Puzzles 1

Rebus puzzles are puzzles that use pictures, letters, and clues to represent words, expressions, and other familiar things. Have some fun with rebus puzzles. Can you figure out the puzzles below?

1. BRIDGE

   WATER

   _____

2. ↑ T
     O
     W
     N

   _____

143

Rebus Puzzles II

Rebus puzzles are puzzles that use pictures, letters, and clues to represent words, expressions, and other familiar things. Below are two rebus puzzles. See if you can solve them.

1. IIIIIIIIIIIIIIIIIIIII
   ──────────────────
   bag   bag   bag

   _____

2. pepperoni
   ─────────
   pizza

   _____

Create Your Own

Rebus puzzles are puzzles that use pictures, letters, and clues to represent words, expressions, and other familiar things. Now it's your turn to make up rebus puzzles. Create two below. Then exchange papers with a partner and see if he or she can solve your puzzles.

145

Crossword Conundrum VIII

The words in this crossword puzzle are all synonyms and antonyms for words that begin with the letter *j*. Solve the puzzle using the clues. You may use a thesaurus if needed.

146

Across

1. a synonym of *jaundiced*
4. a synonym of *joyous*
5. an antonym of *joyous*
6. an antonym of *jeopardy*

Down

2. an antonym of *jaundiced*
3. a synonym of *jeopardy*

"X" Marks the Spot

There are not many words in English that begin with the letter *x*. List as many as you can. Then compare your list with that of a partner. How many did the two of you find altogether?

147

What a Bore!

Liven up the sentences below. Replace each underlined word with a more specific and interesting word. Write your new word on the line before each sentence.

_____ 1. Joaquin <u>sang</u> as Janine played the piano.

_____ 2. Barry <u>looked</u> into the musty old box.

_____ 3. Before eating the wild berries, Allegra <u>smelled</u> them.

_____ 4. Sanjay <u>ran</u> the last few yards to the coffee shop.

_____ 5. Martin <u>drank</u> his juice before the next class began.

148

Pure Nonsense

If you disagree with someone, you might say his or her theory is hokum. How many other words can you list that mean "nonsense"? Make a list below. Then try out your nonsense words on classmates.

149

Quite a Character

Charles Dickens, Roald Dahl, and many other writers use names
that fit the personalities of their characters. Sometimes the
meaning of the name describes the character. Other times, the
sound of the name suggests a quality. For each character described
below, create a name you might use in a story.

1. a happy-go-lucky young woman _____

2. a serious, harsh middle-aged man _____

3. a thoughtful, gentle teen _____

    4. an eight-year-old child who has been raised by wolves _____

    5. a strong-willed but fair teacher _____

150

Pet Names

What is your favorite name for a dog? For a cat? Why? Write the names below. Share your list with classmates. Did anyone have the same names that you wrote?

151

Name Matchup

Names can have specific meanings. For example, the name Rex means "king." What do you think the following names mean? Match each name on the left with its meaning on the right. Write the correct letter on the line.

____ 1. Peter   a. flexible, able-bodied

____ 2. Olympia   b. mountain of the gods

____ 3. Ladonna   c. rock

____ 4. Dolores   d. lady of sorrows

____ 5. Dexter   e. woman

Daily Warm-Ups: Vocabulary Word Play

152

"K" Crossword

There are not many words in English that begin with the letter *k*—but all the answers in this crossword puzzle do. Use the clues to solve the puzzle.

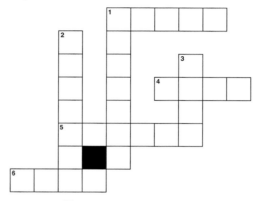

Across

1. praise for achievement
4. structural part that runs along the bottom of a boat
5. fantastic Scandinavian sea monster
6. the strongest part of a castle

Down

1. a yellow or orange citrus fruit with a sweet rind
2. a joint in the fingers
3. to wail for the dead

153

© 2006 Walch Publishing

Money Talks

Think about the money words in the box below. Look them up in a dictionary, if necessary. Then write each word under the correct category.

cheapskate	parsimonious	stingy
closefisted	profligate	thrifty
frugal	spendthrift	wastrel
miser	squanderer	

Spender   **Saver**

154

Where Are You From?

Some proper adjectives tell where someone is from. Sometimes, these adjectives are not exactly what you might expect. See if you can guess where each person listed below is from. Write your answers on the lines.

1. Liverpudlian   _____

2. Cantabrigian   _____

3. Glaswegian   _____

4. Dane   _____

What would you call yourself? Create a proper adjective from the name of your city, town, school, or neighborhood.

155

Quite a Mouthful

Write the longest (real) word you can think of. Share it with classmates. Who wrote the longest word? How many letters does it have? How many syllables? Write your observations below.

156

Monster Madness

Think about some scary books and movies that you have read or seen. Now list as many monsters as you can, such as *zombie* and *mummy*. Create your list below.

157

Stranger Than Fiction

The following words all come from the names of fictional characters. Do you know what each means? Write your answer on the line.

1. grinch _____

2. Pollyanna _____

3. scrooge _____

4. Pecksniffian _____

158

Artful Acrostic

Write an acrostic based on the word below. Try to use fresh, interesting words.

COMMUNITY

Please Clarify

Some words are very similar and are, therefore, easily confused. Circle the word in parentheses that correctly completes each sentence below.

1. It is (all together/ altogether) too cold in here!

2. The bread dough will (raise/rise) overnight.

3. Tell the dog to (lie/lay) down or it will have to go outside.

4. Your apology does not (altar/alter) anything; you still have to go to detention.

160

Bored to Tears

Students often complain of being bored. How many ways can you think of to say *boring*? Write them below.

161

Why Bother?

Younger siblings often annoy older family members. How many ways can you say *bother*? Write them below. Use some on younger brothers or sisters sometime and see if they know what you mean.

162

Language Puzzler

Solve the puzzle using the clues below. All the words are related to language.

```
                              ¹P
                          ²   O
                              ³L
          ⁴                   Y
                          ⁵   G
                              ⁶L
                  ⁷           O
          ⁸                   T
```

1. to say correctly
2. the art of effective public speaking
3. someone who speaks several languages
4. a collection of words
5. a word that is the same in more than one language
6. the vocabulary of a language or group
7. a choice of words
8. one who orally translates from one language to another

163

The Good, the Bad, and the Ugly

Read the words in the box below. Group the words under the correct headings. Then add some of your own words to each list.

corrupt	gorgon	immoral	reprobate
demonic	grotesque	lofty	sinister
depraved	hideous	moral	virtuous
gargoyle	homely	noble	wholesome

GOOD   **BAD**   **UGLY**

164

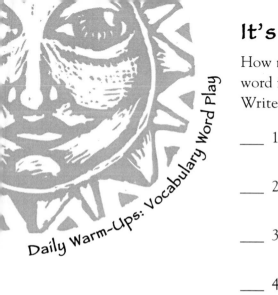

It's All Greek to Me

How much do you know about Greek mythology? Match each word from mythology on the left with its meaning on the right. Write the correct letter on the line.

_____ 1. halcyon

_____ 2. hydra

_____ 3. tantalize

_____ 4. chimerical

a. a many-faceted problem that cannot be fixed with one solution

b. fantastical; possible only in the imagination

c. golden; wonderful

d. to tempt

165

Ad Nauseam

Some words seem to go in and out of style. The word *eclectic*, for example, appears everywhere to describe a mixed-bag style. Think about ads you have seen in magazines or on television. Can you think of a few words that are repeated many times? Write them below. Then copy an advertising slogan using one of those words and substitute another word. Maybe you'll start a new language trend!

166

Quotable Quotes

Abraham Lincoln once said, "He can compress the most words into the smallest ideas of any man I ever met." What do you think he meant? Do you know anyone like that? Rephrase what Lincoln said in your own words.

167

Road to Perdition

In 2002, the movie *Road to Perdition* was released. Write a definition of the word *perdition*. Then explain what you think the meaning of the title is.

168

"S" Crossword

Create a small crossword puzzle using the following words that begin with the letter *s*:

soporific   subjugate

squalid   supplant

stases   swarthy

Draw your puzzle and write the clues on a separate sheet of paper. Then have a classmate complete the puzzle.

169

"M" Crossword

Create a small crossword puzzle using the following words that begin with the letter *m*:

mawkish   motley

mellifluous   multifarious

misanthrope   myriad

Draw your puzzle and write the clues on a separate sheet of paper. Then have a classmate complete the puzzle.

170

Concept Map III

The word *condone* means "to agree with by overlooking."
Complete the concept map below for the word *condone*.

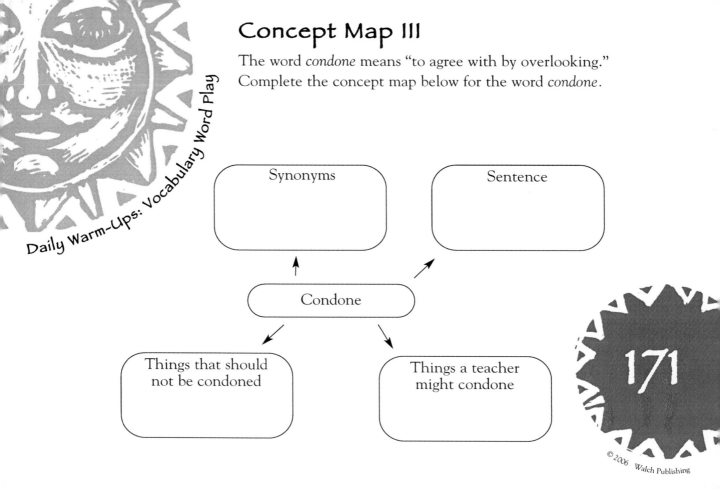

| Synonyms | Sentence |

Condone

Things that should
not be condoned

Things a teacher
might condone

171

Concept Map IV

The word *hedonistic* means "pleasure-seeking" or "wild." Complete the concept map below for the word *hedonistic*.

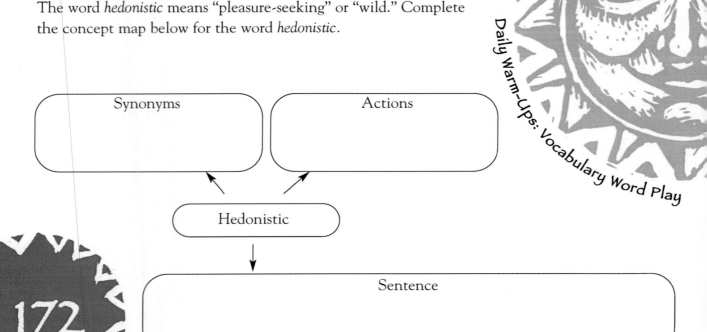

Synonyms

Actions

Hedonistic

Sentence

Let's Talk

Read the words in the box below. The words can be classified as synonyms or antonyms of the word *garrulous*. Write the words in the appropriate columns.

chatty	quiet	understated
concise	taciturn	verbose
discursive	terse	voluble
loquacious		

Synonyms   **Antonyms**

Please Classify

Read the words in the box below. The words can be classified as synonyms or antonyms of the word *abhor*. Write the words in the appropriate columns.

admire	denounce	esteem	loathe
adore	detest	hate	revere

Synonyms **Antonyms**

174

Rearrange It

Rearranging the letters of some words can be fun and revealing. For example, when you rearrange the letters of the word *astronomer*, you get *moon starer*. When you rearrange the letters of the phrase *the Morse code*, you get *here come dots*.

See if you can unscramble a word of your own and come up with a clever new phrase.

175

Proverbial Phrase

An old English proverb says, "Use soft words and hard arguments." What do you think this means? What do you think of this concept? Write your ideas below.

176

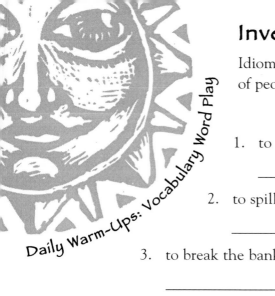

Investigating Idioms

Idioms are phrases or groups of words that are peculiar to a group of people. Write the meaning of each common idiom below.

1. to pull one's leg _____

   _____

2. to spill the beans _____

   _____

3. to break the bank _____

   _____

177

Mythology Crossword

Use the clues to complete the crossword puzzle using words that come from Greek mythology.

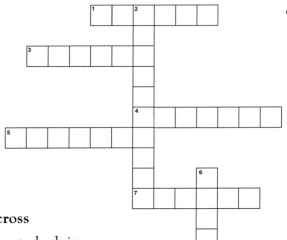

Daily Warm-Ups: Vocabulary Word Play

178

Across

1. a trusted advisor
3. a gentle breeze
4. impassive
5. the Greek goddess of vengeance
7. a place where objects are exhibited
8. a long voyage

Down

2. a love of oneself
6. a kind of shield

All You Need Is Love

All you need for this word search is love. See how many synonyms you can find for the word *love*. There are ten.

```
M Z P G Y F F V N F R I G V M
N D H N H G M O T P V E N M D
F O V L S K I Q F H N F V Z D
J P I I K T Y Y F C O X D R M
B E D T O K G G H L I A V G G
K W M V C C B A C R T O A V S
G Q E O A E N C A I A S C E G
R D H R T T F P W T R O D R A
L I A G M I T F G G O K P Z U
Q N D E D U O O A D D E A I F
W G N O R E W N P T A G S B I
C T Y E A R N I N G B J S K B
N O I T A U T A F N I M I H D
Q X W H U V N H A U R W O O P
B N K Q Q C U K V J Y P N P C
```

179

The Mother of Invention

Think about the following proverb: Necessity is the mother of invention. How does this proverb apply to language? Write your ideas below.

180

1. 1. relish; 2. savory; 3. gorge; 4. digest; 5. season; 6. whisked
2. Explanations will vary. 1. bringing trouble or distress; 2. unnecessary; 3. an introductory statement
3. Answers will vary.
4. Answers will vary.
5. 1. tractor; 2. distractions; 3. retracted; 4. detract; 5. contract; 6. subtract; 7. traction; 8. intractable; 9. extract; 10. protracted
6. Paragraphs will vary.
7. Answers will vary.
8. Answers will vary.
9. Answers will vary. Sample answers: artichokes, broccoli, cucumber, celery, cauliflower, potatoes
10. Answers will vary.
11. Answers will vary.
12. Answers will vary. Sample answers: links, lynx; hair, hare; deer, dear
13. Answers will vary.
14. Answers will vary.
15. Answers will vary. Sample answers: joyous, merry, gleeful, genial, jolly, hilarious, exhilarated, congenial, elated, radiant, jubilant, thrilled
16. 1. the cat's pajamas; 2. raining cats and dogs; 3. horse of a different color; 4. cat got your tongue; 5–6. Answers will vary.
17. 1. c; 2. d; 3. a; 4. f; 5. e; 6. b

Daily Warm-Ups: Vocabulary Word Play

18.

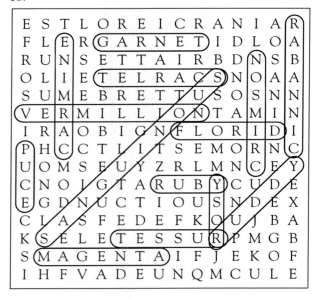

19. 1. torrent; 2. finicky; 3. peril; 4. obstinate;
5. ornate; 6–10. Sentences will vary.
20. 1. blue; 2. red; 3. yellow; 4. blue; 5. green; 6. red;
7. white; 8. gray; 9. brown; 10. black
21. 1. cool; 2. lonely; 3. admiration; 4. display;
5. clean; 6–10. Sentences will vary.
22. EARTH: clod, geology, pumice, terrestrial,
territory
AIR: aerosol, ethereal, pulmonary, respiration
FIRE: char, combustion, ignite, incendiary,
inflammable
WATER: aquatic, condensation, glacial, humidity,
lachrymose, perspiration
23. 1. well; 2. amount; 3. hoard; 4. uninterested;
5. conscious; 6. lose; 7. among; 8. good;
9. eminent; 10. word usage
24. 1. N; 2. P; 3. P; 4. N; 5. P; 6. N; 7. N; 8. P; 9. P;
10. N; 11. N; 12. P; 13. P; 14. P; 15. N; 16. P;
17. N; 18. N

25. 1. star; 2. star; 3. moon; 4. sun; 5. the planet Mercury; Other words will vary.
26. Answers will vary. Sample answers: psychoanalysis, psychic, psychologist, psychotic
27. 1. fear of closed spaces; 2. fear of open spaces; 3. fear of society; 4. fear of books; 5. fear of writing; 6. fear of drugs; 7. fear of birds; 8. fear of words
28. 1. contiguous; 2. stagnate; 3. depression; 4. turbulence; 5. dissipate; 6. saturate; 7–8. Answers will vary.
29. 1. b; 2. d; 3. e; 4. g; 5. h; 6. f; 7. a; 8. c
30. 1. sponge lunge; 2. jungle bungle; 3. stung lung; 4. study buddy; 5. penned friend; 6. sweet treat; 7. slick flick; 8. book crook; 9. king bling; 10. late date; 11–12. Answers will vary.
31. 1. d; 2. e; 3. c; 4. j; 5. i; 6. g; 7. a; 8. b; 9. h; 10. f
32. Answers will vary. Sample answers: 1. fox; 2. cat; 3. dog; 4. mule, donkey; 5. peacock; 6. cow; 7. rat, pig; 8. lamb; 9. cricket; 10. snake

33. Answers will vary. Look for hyperbolic adjectives such as stupendous, extreme, fabulous, and extraordinary.
34. Answers will vary. Sample answers: humdinger, doozy, corker, lulu
35.

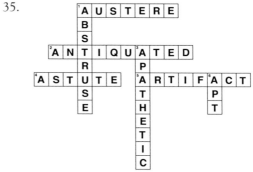

36. 1. get going; 2. make arrangements; 3. tell the truth; 4. lose your temper; 5. be attractive to someone; 6–7. Answers will vary.
37. Answers will vary.

Daily Warm-Ups: Vocabulary Word Play

38.

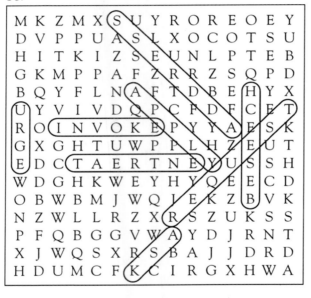

39. Answers will vary. Sample answers: assert, adopt, cherish, avow, claim, defend, hold, proclaim, uphold, retain, maintain

40. Answers will vary. Sample answers: dad, did, deed, civic, sees, Otto

41. Answers will vary. Sample answers: boycott, sideburns, derringer

42. 1. mule; 2. yen; 3. chuck; 4. vault; Homographs will vary.

43. 1. content; 2. object; 3. intimate; 4. refuse; Heteronyms will vary.

44. 1. cleave; 2. sanction; 3. fast; 4. oversight

45. Answers will vary. Sample answers: thingamabob, thingamajig, doohickey, doodad, watchamacallit, whatzit

Answer Key

46.

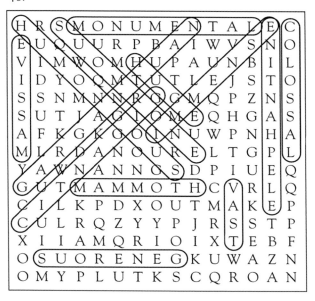

47. 1. activities; 2. videos; 3. teeth; 4. loaves;
    5. heroes; 6. women; 7. oxen; 8. geese; 9. media;
    10. bases; 11. families; 12. turkeys; 13. waltzes
48. Answers will vary.
49. Answers will vary.
50. Answers will vary.
51. 1. airplane; 2. alligator; 3. hosiery; 4. umpire;
    5. helicopter; 6. memorandum; 7. refrigerator;
    8. chimpanzee

Daily Warm-Ups: Vocabulary Word Play

52.

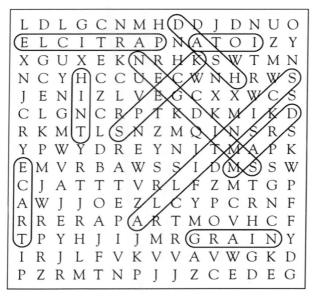

53.

```
        ¹L                    ⁹S
        I          ³M    ⁴L    P
     ⁵P G          E     U     E
      U I          L     M     C
     ⁶U L T R A V I O L E T    T
      P N          A     N     R
      I I          N     O     U
      L N          I     U     M
        G          N     S
                         S
```

54. 1. laughable; 2. courtship; 3. gloomy; 4. obscene;
    5. lonely; 6. dwindle; 7. excellent; 8. premeditated

55. Puzzles will vary.

56. 1. photo; 2. trans; 3. semi; 4. micro; 5. inter;
    6. pseudo; 7. under; 8. super; Examples will vary.
    Where does a prefix go? It PRECEDES a word.

57. 1. bacterium; 2. cherubim; 3. datum; 4. crisis;
    5. wolf; 6. sheep; 7. beau; 8. criterion;
    9. phenomenon; 10. son-in-law

58. 1. lies; 2. bloom; 3. giant; 4. hate; 5. part; 6. slid;
    7. male

59. Answers will vary. Sample answers: walk: saunter,

stroll, tramp, trudge, hike; courage: valor, bravery, grit, pluck, mettle

60.

```
¹P R E N ²A T A L
O       N
²S   ³A N T E D I L U V I A N
T       E
H       B
U   ⁴P R E N U P T I A L
M       L
O       L
U       U
S   ⁵S I M U L T A N E O U S
```

61.

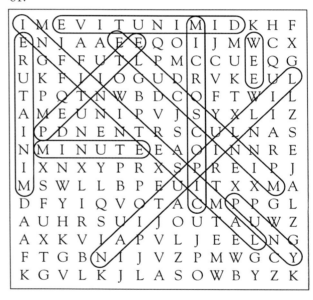

62. 1. bib; 2. gag; 3. civic; 4. kayak; 5. wow; 6. dad;
     7. radar; 8. did
63. 1. c; 2. g; 3. e; 4. f; 5. a; 6. b; 7. d
64.

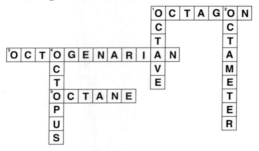

65. Puzzles will vary.

66.

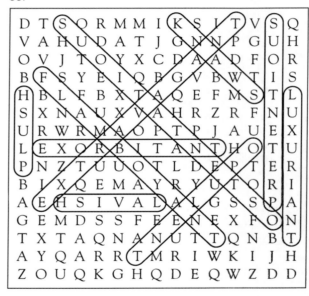

67.

68. Answers will vary. Sample answers: 1. bronchitis; 2. gastronomy; 3. chemotherapy; 4. hemoglobin; 5. archaeologist; 6. microscopic

69. Answers will vary. Sample answers: sorrowful, glum, pensive, dismal, downcast, troubled, unhappy, gloomy, depressed, desolate, dejected

70. All are musical instruments.

71.

72. Answers will vary. Sample answers: description, postscript, prescription, subscription, typescript, nondescript

73. Answers will vary. Sample answers: whisper, mumble, assert, shout, pronounce, utter

74. Answers will vary.

75. Answers will vary. Sample answers: 1. unfair; 2. evil; 3. ending; 4. outgoing; 5. lasting; 6. refreshed; 7. aware; 8. large

76.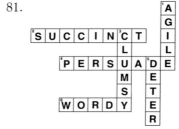

77. Answers will vary. Sample answers: 1. lie;
    2. useless; 3. poor; 4. sleepy; 5. persistence;
    6. cruel; 7. fear; 8. panacea

78. b; Sentences will vary.

79. c; Sentences will vary.

80. c; Sentences will vary.

81.

82.

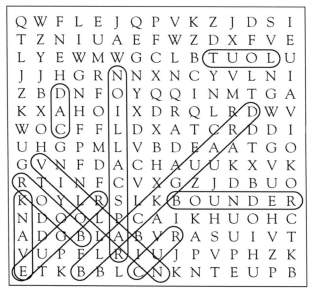

83. c; Sentences will vary.
84. All words are related to food. Sentences will vary.

85. Answers will vary. Sample answers: new innovation, lonely isolation, free gift, pair of twins

86.

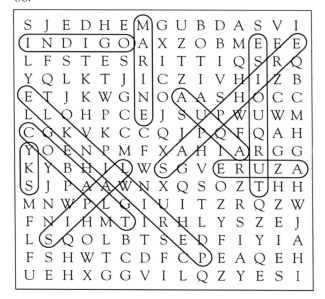

Daily Warm-Ups: Vocabulary Word Play

87.

```
M I L D
      E
      F
T R U C U L E N T
  O         A
  B         T
  U     W
  S U C C E S S
  T     A
        K
```

88. 1. nonporous; 2. impertinent; 3. irrelevant;
4. discontent; 5. unguarded; 6. illegible; Sentences
will vary.

89. 1. charge; 2. literate; 3. mobilize; 4. resolute;
5. fiction; 6. fertile; Sentences will vary.

90. 1. paparazzi; 2. cacophony; 3. correct;
4. discombobulate; 5. correct; 6. abundant;
7. entrepreneur; 8. meringue

91. 1. incision; 2. constituents; Sentences will vary.

92.

```
P
I     A B R U P T   V
E     R             O
C   D A S T A R D L Y
E     R             U
M     I             B
E     V             L
A     E
I N A R T I C U L A T E
L
```

93. Answers will vary.

94. Answers will vary. Sample answers: sup, supper,
port, able, portable, table, pot, pore, part, store,
sable, support, stable, unstable, pun, punt, blip,
pus, bun, pin, pint, plus, stop

95. Answers will vary.

96. Answers will vary.

97. Answers will vary.

98. Answers will vary.

99. Cartoons will vary. Sample revised sentences:
With the cat yowling, do you have a problem
talking on the phone?

Walking through the garden, I smelled the flowers.
Chasing his tail, the dog ran after the boy.
Gripping the microphone stand, the singer hit the high note.

100. 1. b; 2. a; 3. b; 4. b; 5. a; Questions will vary.
101. Answers will vary.
102. Answers will vary.
103.

104. Answers will vary.
105. Answers will vary.
106. Answers will vary.
107. Answers will vary.
108. Answers will vary.
109. Answers will vary.
110. Answers will vary.
111. Answers will vary.
112. Answers will vary.
113. 1. f; 2. b; 3. a; 4. e; 5. g; 6. c; 7. d
114. 1. d; 2. h; 3. c; 4. b; 5. a; 6. f; 7. g; 8. e; Sentences will vary.
115. 1. an argument against; 2. smuggled goods; 3. a violation; 4. ordinary; 5. incapable of being perceived; Made-up definitions will vary.
116. 1. d; 2. e; 3. a; 4. h; 5. b; 6. i; 7. c; 8. f; 9. g
117. Answers will vary. Sample answers: acne, acre, care, cane, cure, earn, lane, lance, lava, naval, navel, near, rave, rare, racer, rule, ulcer, uncle, value

Daily Warm-Ups: Vocabulary Word Play

118. 1. cinquain; 2. secondary; 3. biped;
     4. septuagenarian; 5. centipede; 6. Pentagon;
     7. biennial; 8. uniform; 9. tercentennial;
     10. bipartisan

119. Answers will vary.

120. Answers will vary. Sample answer: High-sounding
     words: inalienable rights, independence, equality,
     representation, diplomacy, democracy; High-
     minded actions: granting voting rights for women,
     showing respect for differences, finding a way to
     fairly represent the different states, providing true
     equality under the law, using speeches and wit
     rather than violence to solve problems, acting
     rather than just talking

121. Answers will vary.

122. Answers will vary.

123.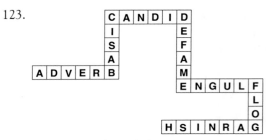

124. 1. e; 2. a; 3. b; 4. d; 5. c

125. Answers will vary. Real definitions: 1. to shrink
     from drying up; The diminutive is *crinkle*; 2. to
     waste away; The diminutive is *drindle*; 3. to weep
     in anger (rather than in sorrow); 4. to complain;
     5. to grow old

126. 1. a; 2. d; 3. b; 4. e; 5. c

127. 1. distress, mortification; 2. imitation, usually
     inferior; 3. one who takes the law into his or her
     own hands, usually in revenge for a specific crime;
     4. (adj.) relating to a suicide mission; 5. spirit,
     vitality

128. Answers will vary. Real definitions: 1. restless;
2. quarrelsome; 3. heavy, difficult to move; 4. hot
and stuffy; 5. unreasonable (in arguments)

129. 1. happiness; 2. fifth son; 3. bailiff, steward;
4. white; 5. assistant

130. Answers will vary.

131. Answers will vary.

132. Answers will vary. Sample answers: 1. engaged,
interested; 2. agitated, enervated,
discombobulated; 3. sad, dejected; 4. depressed,
miserable

133. Answers will vary.

134. 1. b; 2. d; 3. c; 4. a;

135. Answers will vary.

136. Answers will vary.

137. Answers will vary.

138.

```
D C S Z O F R R E C V Q C V J
A E Z K N K E R O X I G L B R
Q R L C C D N G O K G X H Z M
U E B I N M I Q N P E D P T P
I B X O B T E Q W Z T S Y G Q
E R P I A E R T U X A L H C M
D A I T E R I A V X E B X N
B T E O F H Z A L N A X D B V
R E D I S N O C T N I L Z B T
L H Y B B T R M C E C M S R C
A E H N S O Y L M W M P U N E
C O N T E M P L A T E U L R L
V O W E I G H P Q W P Y S J F
F C C H Q O Z G A T K A Y E E
S W D O I S M Z X R D V G G R
```

Daily Warm-Ups: Vocabulary Word Play

139.

140. 1. c; 2. a; 3. b

141. Answers will vary. Sample answers: bite the big one, the big sleep, breathe one's last, cash out, crossing the bar, end of the line, flatline

142. 1. b; 2. c; 3. c; 4. c; 5. c; Sentences will vary.

143. 1. water under the bridge; 2. uptown

144. 1. bags under the eyes; 2. pizza with pepperoni on top

145. Puzzles will vary.

146.

147. Answers will vary.

148. Answers will vary. Sample answers: 1. crooned; 2. peered; 3. sniffed; 4. trotted; 5. gulped

149. Answers will vary. Sample answers: gobbledygook, codswallop, blarney, malarkey, baloney

150. Answers will vary.

151. Answers will vary.

152. 1. c; 2. b; 3. e; 4. d; 5. a

153.

```
        ¹K U D O S
   ²K    U
    N    M      ³K
    U    Q   ⁴K E E L
    C    U      E
   ⁵K R A K E N
    L  ■  T
 ⁶K E E P
```

154. Spender: profligate, spendthrift, squanderer, wastrel; Saver: cheapskate, closefisted, frugal, miser, parsimonious, stingy, thrifty

155. 1. Liverpool, England; 2. Cambridge, Massachusetts; 3. Glasgow, Scotland; 4. Denmark; Adjectives will vary.

156. Answers will vary.

157. Answers will vary.

158. 1. a mean-spirited grouch; 2. someone who is annoyingly optimistic; 3. a hoarder; 4. hypocritical

159. Answers will vary.

160. 1. altogether; 2. rise; 3. lie; 4. alter

161. Answers will vary. Sample answers: dull, mundane, tedious, soporific, insipid, ho-hum, bland, dry

162. Answers will vary. Sample answers: pester, hector, vex, pique, try, irritate, peeve

163. 1. pronounce; 2. elocution; 3. linguist; 4. vocabulary; 5. cognate; 6. lexicon; 7. diction; 8. interpreter

164. GOOD: lofty, moral, noble, virtuous, wholesome
BAD: corrupt, demonic, depraved, immoral, reprobate, sinister
UGLY: gargoyle, gorgon, grotesque, hideous, homely

165. 1. c; 2. a; 3. d; 4. b

166. Answers will vary. You may wish to have some magazines available for students to look at in class, or have students bring in materials from home.

167. Answers will vary. Students may observe that Lincoln was commenting on someone who seemed to talk a lot without saying anything meaningful.

168. *Perdition* refers to eternal damnation. Explanations will vary.
169. Puzzles will vary.
170. Puzzles will vary.
171. Answers will vary.
172. Answers will vary.
173. Synonyms: chatty, discursive, loquacious, verbose, voluble; Antonyms: concise, quiet, terse, taciturn, understated
174. Synonyms: denounce, detest, hate, loathe
     Antonyms: admire, adore, esteem, revere
175. Answers will vary.
176. Answers will vary.
177. 1. to be fooling; to be exaggerating; 2. to tell a secret; 3. to spend all one's money

178.

```
        ¹M E ²N T O R
            A
  ³Z E P H Y R
            C
            I
          ⁴S T O I C A L
  ⁵N E M E S I S
            I
            S        ⁶A
          ⁷M U S E U M
                     G
                     I
  ⁸O D Y S S E Y
```

179.

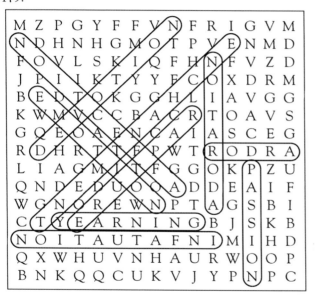

180. Answers will vary.

Daily Warm-Ups: Vocabulary Word Play

Turn downtime into learning time!

For information on other titles in the

Daily *Warm-Ups* series,

visit our web site: walch.com